LET GOD

Being confident of this, that he who began a good work in you will carry it on to completion until the day of Christ Jesus.
Philippians 1:6

_____

_____

_____

_____

_____

_____

_____

_____

_____

_____

_____

_____

_____

_____

_____

_____

_____

_____

_____

_____

_____

_____

_____

_____

The Lord makes firm the steps of the one who delights in him.
Psalm 37:23

_____

_____

_____

_____

_____

_____

_____

_____

_____

_____

_____

_____

_____

_____

_____

_____

_____

_____

_____

_____

_____

_____

_____

_____

The Lord replied, 'My Presence will go with you,
and I will give you rest.'
Exodus 33:14

He heals the brokenhearted and binds up their wounds.
Psalm 147:3

_____

_____

_____

_____

_____

_____

_____

_____

_____

_____

_____

_____

_____

_____

_____

_____

_____

_____

_____

_____

_____

_____

_____

_____

_____

_____

My grace is sufficient for you,
for my power is made perfect in weakness.
2 Corinthians 12:9

_____

_____

_____

_____

_____

_____

_____

_____

_____

_____

_____

_____

_____

_____

_____

_____

_____

_____

_____

_____

_____

_____

_____

_____

But seek first his kingdom and his righteousness,
and all these things will be given to you as well.
Matthew 6:33

_____

_____

_____

_____

_____

_____

_____

_____

_____

_____

_____

_____

_____

_____

_____

_____

_____

_____

_____

_____

_____

_____

_____

_____

Though your sins are like scarlet, they shall be as white as snow.
Isaiah 1:18

_____

_____

_____

_____

_____

_____

_____

_____

_____

_____

_____

_____

_____

_____

_____

_____

_____

_____

_____

_____

_____

_____

_____

If we confess our sins, he is faithful and just and
will forgive us our sins and purify us from all unrighteousness.
1 John 1:9

_____

_____

_____

_____

_____

_____

_____

_____

_____

_____

_____

_____

_____

_____

_____

_____

_____

_____

_____

_____

_____

_____

_____

_____

He said to me: 'It is done. I am the Alpha and the Omega,
the Beginning and the End.'
Revelation 21:6

So is my word that goes out from my mouth:
It will not return to me empty.
Isaiah 55:11

_____

_____

_____

_____

_____

_____

_____

_____

_____

_____

_____

_____

_____

_____

_____

_____

_____

_____

_____

_____

_____

_____

_____

_____

_____

I will repay you for the years the locusts have eaten.
Joel 2:25

_____

_____

_____

_____

_____

_____

_____

_____

_____

_____

_____

_____

_____

_____

_____

_____

_____

_____

_____

_____

_____

_____

_____

_____

And the God of all grace... will himself restore you
and make you strong, firm and steadfast.
1 Peter 5:10

_____

_____

_____

_____

_____

_____

_____

_____

_____

_____

_____

_____

_____

_____

_____

_____

_____

_____

_____

_____

_____

_____

_____

_____

_____

Lord, you alone are my portion and my cup;
you make my lot secure.
Psalm 16:5–6

_____

_____

_____

_____

_____

_____

_____

_____

_____

_____

_____

_____

_____

_____

_____

_____

_____

_____

_____

_____

_____

_____

The Lord will fight for you; you need only to be still.
Exodus 14:14

_____

_____

_____

_____

_____

_____

_____

_____

_____

_____

_____

_____

_____

_____

_____

_____

_____

_____

_____

_____

_____

_____

_____

_____

If God is for us, who can be against us?
Romans 8:31

_____

_____

_____

_____

_____

_____

_____

_____

_____

_____

_____

_____

_____

_____

_____

_____

_____

_____

_____

_____

_____

_____

_____

_____

Look at the nations and watch—and be utterly amazed.
Habakkuk 1:5

My son, do not despise the Lord's discipline...
because the Lord disciplines those he loves.
Proverbs 3:11–12

_____

_____

_____

_____

_____

_____

_____

_____

_____

_____

_____

_____

_____

_____

_____

_____

_____

_____

_____

_____

_____

_____

_____

_____

Search me, God, and know my heart;
test me and know my anxious thoughts.
Psalm 139:23–24

Those who cleanse themselves…
will be instruments for special purposes, made holy.
2 Timothy 2:21

_____

_____

_____

_____

_____

_____

_____

_____

_____

_____

_____

_____

_____

_____

_____

_____

_____

_____

_____

_____

_____

_____

_____

_____

*Let perseverance finish its work so that
you may be mature and complete.
James 1:4*

_____

_____

_____

_____

_____

_____

_____

_____

_____

_____

_____

_____

_____

_____

_____

_____

_____

_____

_____

_____

_____

_____

_____

_____

Let us not become weary in doing good,
for at the proper time we will reap a harvest.
Galatians 6:9

_____

_____

_____

_____

_____

_____

_____

_____

_____

_____

_____

_____

_____

_____

_____

_____

_____

_____

_____

_____

_____

_____

_____

_____

_____

_____

He says, 'Be still, and know that I am God.'
Psalm 46:10

_____

_____

_____

_____

_____

_____

_____

_____

_____

_____

_____

_____

_____

_____

_____

_____

_____

_____

_____

_____

_____

_____

_____

_____

But those who hope in the Lord will renew their strength.
Isaiah 40:31

_____

_____

_____

_____

_____

_____

_____

_____

_____

_____

_____

_____

_____

_____

_____

_____

_____

_____

_____

_____

_____

_____

_____

_____

Though outwardly we are wasting away,
yet inwardly we are being renewed day by day.
2 Corinthians 4:16

_____

_____

_____

_____

_____

_____

_____

_____

_____

_____

_____

_____

_____

_____

_____

_____

_____

_____

_____

_____

_____

_____

_____

_____

Praise be to the Lord, to God our Savior,
who daily bears our burdens.
Psalm 68:19

Do not conform to the pattern of this world,
but be transformed by the renewing of your mind.
Romans 12:2

_____

_____

_____

_____

_____

_____

_____

_____

_____

_____

_____

_____

_____

_____

_____

_____

_____

_____

_____

_____

_____

_____

_____

*For it is God who works in you to will and to act
in order to fulfill his good purpose.*
Philippians 2:13

_____

_____

_____

_____

_____

_____

_____

_____

_____

_____

_____

_____

_____

_____

_____

_____

_____

_____

_____

_____

_____

_____

_____

_____

I will remove from them their heart of stone
and give them a heart of flesh.
Ezekiel 11:19

_____

_____

_____

_____

_____

_____

_____

_____

_____

_____

_____

_____

_____

_____

_____

_____

_____

_____

_____

_____

_____

_____

_____

_____

But you are a chosen people, a royal priesthood, a holy nation.
1 Peter 2:9

_____

_____

_____

_____

_____

_____

_____

_____

_____

_____

_____

_____

_____

_____

_____

_____

_____

_____

_____

_____

_____

_____

_____

_____

If anyone is in Christ, the new creation has come.
2 Corinthians 5:17

_____

_____

_____

_____

_____

_____

_____

_____

_____

_____

_____

_____

_____

_____

_____

_____

_____

_____

_____

_____

_____

_____

_____

_____

In their hearts humans plan their course,
but the Lord establishes their steps.
Proverbs 16:9

_____

_____

_____

_____

_____

_____

_____

_____

_____

_____

_____

_____

_____

_____

_____

_____

_____

_____

_____

_____

_____

_____

_____

And the peace of God, which transcends all understanding,
will guard your hearts and your minds in Christ Jesus.
Philippians 4:7

Let the peace of Christ rule in your hearts,
since as members of one body you were called to peace.
Colossians 3:15

_____

_____

_____

_____

_____

_____

_____

_____

_____

_____

_____

_____

_____

_____

_____

_____

_____

_____

_____

_____

_____

_____

_____

_____

_____

_____

You intended to harm me, but God intended it for good
to accomplish what is now being done.
Genesis 50:20

_____

_____

_____

_____

_____

_____

_____

_____

_____

_____

_____

_____

_____

_____

_____

_____

_____

_____

_____

_____

_____

_____

_____

_____

_____

I am the Alpha and the Omega,
who is, and who was, and who is to come, the Almighty.
Revelation 1:8

_____

_____

_____

_____

_____

_____

_____

_____

_____

_____

_____

_____

_____

_____

_____

_____

_____

_____

_____

_____

_____

_____

_____

_____

But the plans of the Lord stand firm forever,
the purposes of his heart through all generations.
Psalm 33:11

_____

_____

_____

_____

_____

_____

_____

_____

_____

_____

_____

_____

_____

_____

_____

_____

_____

_____

_____

_____

_____

_____

_____

_____

Humble yourselves before the Lord, and he will lift you up.
James 4:10

_____

_____

_____

_____

_____

_____

_____

_____

_____

_____

_____

_____

_____

_____

_____

_____

_____

_____

_____

_____

_____

_____

_____

_____

Dear friends, let us love one another, for love comes from God.
1 John 4:7–8

A new command I give you: Love one another.
As I have loved you, so you must love one another.
John 13:34–35

_____

_____

_____

_____

_____

_____

_____

_____

_____

_____

_____

_____

_____

_____

_____

_____

_____

_____

_____

_____

_____

_____

_____

Blessed are the peacemakers, for they will be called children of God.
Matthew 5:9

_____

_____

_____

_____

_____

_____

_____

_____

_____

_____

_____

_____

_____

_____

_____

_____

_____

_____

_____

_____

_____

_____

_____

_____

Weeping may stay for the night,
but rejoicing comes in the morning.
Psalm 30:5

_____

_____

_____

_____

_____

_____

_____

_____

_____

_____

_____

_____

_____

_____

_____

_____

_____

_____

_____

_____

_____

_____

_____

_____

_____

_____

Do not grieve, for the joy of the Lord is your strength.
Nehemiah 8:10

_____

_____

_____

_____

_____

_____

_____

_____

_____

_____

_____

_____

_____

_____

_____

_____

_____

_____

_____

_____

_____

_____

_____

_____

Commit to the Lord whatever you do,
and he will establish your plans.
Proverbs 16:3

_____

_____

_____

_____

_____

_____

_____

_____

_____

_____

_____

_____

_____

_____

_____

_____

_____

_____

_____

_____

_____

_____

_____

_____

_____

_____

You will keep in perfect peace those whose minds are steadfast,
because they trust in you.
Isaiah 26:3

_____
_____
_____
_____
_____
_____
_____
_____
_____
_____
_____
_____
_____
_____
_____
_____
_____
_____
_____
_____
_____
_____
_____
_____
_____
_____

For the Spirit God gave us does not make us timid,
but gives us power, love and self-discipline.
2 Timothy 1:7

I will place on his shoulder the key to the house of David;
what he opens no one can shut.
Isaiah 22:22

_____

_____

_____

_____

_____

_____

_____

_____

_____

_____

_____

_____

_____

_____

_____

_____

_____

_____

_____

_____

_____

_____

_____

Now faith is confidence in what we hope for
and assurance about what we do not see.
Hebrews 11:1

_____

_____

_____

_____

_____

_____

_____

_____

_____

_____

_____

_____

_____

_____

_____

_____

_____

_____

_____

_____

_____

_____

_____

Immediately the boy's father exclaimed,
'I do believe; help me overcome my unbelief!'
Mark 9:24

_____

_____

_____

_____

_____

_____

_____

_____

_____

_____

_____

_____

_____

_____

_____

_____

_____

_____

_____

_____

_____

_____

_____

*Therefore, there is now no condemnation
for those who are in Christ Jesus.
Romans 8:1*

_____

_____

_____

_____

_____

_____

_____

_____

_____

_____

_____

_____

_____

_____

_____

_____

_____

_____

_____

_____

_____

_____

_____

_____

_____

Above all else, guard your heart,
for everything you do flows from it.
Proverbs 4:23

Put on the full armor of God,
so that you can take your stand against the devil's schemes.
Ephesians 6:10–11

_____

_____

_____

_____

_____

_____

_____

_____

_____

_____

_____

_____

_____

_____

_____

_____

_____

_____

_____

_____

_____

_____

_____

_____

So if the Son sets you free, you will be free indeed.
John 8:36

These have come so that the proven genuineness of your faith
of greater worth than gold, may result in praise,
glory and honor when Jesus Christ is revealed.
1 Peter 1:7

*Not only so, but we also glory in our sufferings,
because we know that suffering produces perseverance;
perseverance, character; and character, hope.
Romans 5:3–5*

_____

_____

_____

_____

_____

_____

_____

_____

_____

_____

_____

_____

_____

_____

_____

_____

_____

_____

_____

_____

_____

_____

_____

_____

When Jesus spoke again to the people, he said,
'I am the light of the world. Whoever follows me will never walk in
darkness, but will have the light of life.'
John 8:12

Do not conform to the pattern of this world,
but be transformed by the renewing of your mind.
Romans 12:2

_____

_____

_____

_____

_____

_____

_____

_____

_____

_____

_____

_____

_____

_____

_____

_____

_____

_____

_____

_____

_____

_____

Whatever is true, whatever is noble, whatever is right,
whatever is pure, whatever is lovely, whatever is admirable,
think about such things.
Philippians 4:8

_____

_____

_____

_____

_____

_____

_____

_____

_____

_____

_____

_____

_____

_____

_____

_____

_____

_____

_____

_____

_____

_____

_____

_____

_____

_____

Because of the Lord's great love we are not consumed,
for his compassions never fail. They are new every morning.
Lamentations 3:22–23

_____

_____

_____

_____

_____

_____

_____

_____

_____

_____

_____

_____

_____

_____

_____

_____

_____

_____

_____

_____

_____

_____

_____

_____

Yet I will rejoice in the Lord, I will be joyful in God my Savior.
Habakkuk 3:18–19

_____

_____

_____

_____

_____

_____

_____

_____

_____

_____

_____

_____

_____

_____

_____

_____

_____

_____

_____

_____

_____

_____

_____

_____

And whatever you do, whether in word or deed,
do it all in the name of the Lord Jesus.
Colossians 3:17

_____

_____

_____

_____

_____

_____

_____

_____

_____

_____

_____

_____

_____

_____

_____

_____

_____

_____

_____

_____

_____

_____

_____

*"Let your light shine before others,
that they may see your good deeds and
glorify your Father in heaven."*
Matthew 5:16

Shine Your Light!

yourlightwithin.app

Your Light Within

www.ingramcontent.com/pod-product-compliance
Lightning Source LLC
Chambersburg PA
CBHW070627130626
46555CB00006B/2465